50 THINGS TO KNOW ABOUT BABYSITTING IN YOUR HOME

Bonnie Byler

50 Things to Know

50 Things to Know About Babysitting in Your Home Copyright © 2018 by CZYK Publishing LLC. All Rights Reserved.

All rights reserved. No part of this book may be reproduced in any form or by any electronic or mechanical means including information storage and retrieval systems, without permission in writing from the author. The only exception is by a reviewer, who may quote short excerpts in a review.

Cover designed by: Ivana Stamenkovic
Cover Image: https://pixabay.com/en/nursery-crib-chair-bedroom-room-1078923/

CZYK Publishing Since 2011.

50 Things to Know
Visit our website at www.50thingstoknow..com

Lock Haven, PA
All rights reserved.
ISBN: 9781723901652

50 THINGS TO KNOW ABOUT BABYSITTING IN YOUR HOME

50 Things to Know

BOOK DESCRIPTION

Have you ever thought of babysitting in your home?
Do you wonder what you need to know to legally and safely care for children?

Do you want some ideas about how to be successful with parents and children as a babysitter?

If you answered yes to any of these questions then this book is for you.

50 things to know about babysitting in your home by Bonnie Byler offers a comprehensive approach to caring for children while running a business. Most books on babysitting at home tell you to the very basic ways to monitor kids, keep them busy, and get through the day. Although there's nothing wrong with that as a start, there is so much more to know before you even get started.

Based on knowledge from the world's leading experts, a full-time babysitter will spend as much or more time with a child as its parents. This means that you are not just responsible for watching these children, you are helping raise them.

In these pages you'll discover ways to make sure that you are you and the families you help are both protected. You will also learn what speedbumps you may encounter and how to help prevent many of them. This book will help you develop a plan for building your business, engaging with parents and children, keeping everyone safe and healthy, and handling any issues that may arise.

By the time you finish this book, you will know more than just how to get through the day with babysitting. You will know what to expect, how to handle it, and how to be successful in your business and your role as a child care provider. So grab YOUR copy today. You'll be glad you did.

TABLE OF CONTENTS

50 Things to Know
Book Series
Reviews from Readers
BOOK DESCRIPTION
TABLE OF CONTENTS
DEDICATION
ABOUT THE AUTHOR
INTRODUCTION
1. Know The Laws
2. How Much Will You Charge?
3. CPR
4. Assistance
5. Background Check
6. Decide Your Availability
7. Home Schooling/Homebound
8. Menu
9. Allergies
10. Paperwork
11. Discounts/Other Fees
12. Childproofing Your Home
13. First Aid Kit
14. Toys and Activities
15. Food Labeling and Storage
16. Treat and Reward System

50 Things to Know

17. Nap Areas and Supplies
18. Overnights?
19. Lesson Plans
20. Extra Clothes
21. Discipline
22. Getting Paid
23. Behavior Management - Discipline/Rewards
24. Field Trips
25. Outside Playtime
26. Homework
27. Car Seats and Transportation
28. If You Have Pets
29. Meet Your New Friends
30. "I Don't Have To"
31. "I'm Bored"
32. Lice and Bedbugs
33. Group Projects
34. Update Letters or Emails
35. Damage Policies
36. Plan For An Emergency
37. Demonstrate Structure
38. Decorate Your Space
39. Know When To Call
40. Scheduling Days Off
41. Problem Children
42. Problem Parents

43. Pacifiers and Bottles
44. What Do They Want From You?
45. Ask For References
46. Home Life
47. People Who Cannot Pick Up The Child
48. Renewal Time
49. Discharging a Client
50. Don't Forget To Bond

50 Things to Know

50 Things to Know

DEDICATION

This book is dedicated to my mother. She spent my childhood babysitting and raising us as individuals. She taught me to recognize the spark in every child and to nurture it in the way each child needs. There is no true guide to raising children but she gave me a full and meaningful foundation on which I have built my own family. She continues to teach me to this day.

ns to Know

ABOUT THE AUTHOR

Bonnie is a mother of six and has degrees in Psychology and in Communication. She has been raising her children for 23 years and was a babysitter from the age of 13. She continues to assist parents with raising their children through babysitting and advice.

She is currently a daily mother and writer, freelancing from home.

You can find her on Twitter @bonniebell. Please follow her for more positivity, information, comedy and tips for life as we walk through it.

50 Things to Know

INTRODUCTION

"Children do not care how much you know until they know how much you care."

-Teddy Roosevelt

Many people think of babysitting at home as a way to make a few dollars and nothing more. The reality is that you are doing much more than that when you make the decision to start your own business caring for other people's children.

In addition to setting up your environment to be conducive to safety and fun, you also need to think about the many legal aspects of your choice. There is licensing, paperwork, accounting, safety, health, education, and more!

In this book, I will give you 50 tips that will prepare you to take this leap into working from home and taking care of children. You will be ready to start earning money and helping families to raise their bundles of joy when they are not able to be there. Let's take a look at some of the things you are going to want to think about.

50 Things to Know

1. KNOW THE LAWS

Every state and locality is different. While there are basics about safety and medical care, you can find a lot of variables from place to place. There are rules about how many children per adult or whether you need various licenses such as a business license or possibly health department check-ins. Your space may also be an issue: Do you have to dedicate an area of the home? Is there a size requirement in square feet? It's important to do this research before you set up your plan.

2. HOW MUCH WILL YOU CHARGE?

There are many ways to decide how much you will charge for your services. The best way to start is through research and planning. You will want to look around locally to see what some of your competition is charging.

In order to make your business venture a successful one, you have to be able to survive on your income. Take into consideration things like additional food, utilities, first-aid supplies, and other things you will have to update to be properly set up for children in your home.

You also need to figure out how many children you realistically will *need* to have in your care in order to make your bills. Crunch those numbers and divide it up by the number of families you think you can responsibly handle and you will arrive at your first figure. Now you have a jumping off point and can find the tweaks you may need to make in order to have a rate per child that is reasonable for you and for your prospective clients.

3. CPR

Do you know what to do if someone is choking? How about when to call an ambulance? If you don't know how to protect a life, then you are not ready to accept responsibility for one! Almost every local hospital offers CPR classes and many are free. This is a very important skill to have even if you are not babysitting, so sign up today!

4. ASSISTANCE

Not only for you, but also for your clients, there are many forms of assistance available in the child care industry. Some of the families you work with may be struggling and participating in a program that offers child care assistance but only to those who are licensed by the state. Consider researching and applying for licensing so that you can accept these clients! Often, they are the most in need of a reliable and trustworthy caregiver. Not everyone accepts this assistance so it would be a great way to welcome some lovely people who are looking for someone just like you!

In addition, there are nutritional assistance programs through local Social Services or Health Departments. These programs are designed to assist caregivers with making sure they are able to provide nutritious, delicious snacks and meals to the children in their homes. This is not necessarily need-based, but more of a benefit available to those doing this work and the families they serve. Look into it!

5. BACKGROUND CHECK

This is something a lot of parents will appreciate and it is also required in some states! No one wants to mess around wondering if the person the pulled out of the paper is a criminal or weirdo. Having this to offer a parent can be very reassuring. A simple web search will point you to many companies that offer this service.

Be careful! There are always scams out there and with a background check, you are offering up your personal identification details. If you are unsure **at all**, just go down to the local police department or Social Services office to ask for a referral.

6. DECIDE YOUR AVAILABILITY

Do you want to do full-time? Do you want to work every day? One of the big benefits of babysitting in your own home is that you decide your hours. For full-time, it is traditional to consider before and after school hours, whether you will put them on/take them off the bus, be available as an emergency contact for school and more.

If the children are too young for that, will you be available very early to very late? Make this decision ahead of time so you don't find yourself wavering on the spot and making a commitment you may not be able to keep. This will also help you develop a concise advertisement when the time comes.

7. HOME SCHOOLING/HOMEBOUND

There is a market for this, as well! If you are an educator or even someone who wants to give it a shot, consider offering homeschooling as one of your availabilities. Homebound is another situation in which a child is unable to attend school for one reason or another (medical leave, physical injury, emotional distress, or a number of other reasons).

Some parents wish they could have their children taught in a home environment but are not able to do the job. It may be financial reasons or they may not be confident with the task, but an offering of this nature can bring in a host of clients that are very specifically on the market for this.

Be aware: This gives you the option to charge more per child, but is a massive responsibility. Make sure you are both qualified and interested in this before offering it.

8. MENU

It is important to decide what you will offer in the way of food. In today's world, children have many diet restrictions and it is sometimes better to require parents to provide their own snacks and meals. However, it is a big attraction to parents when that is taken care of and they do not have to handle it each morning while they are rushing around getting ready for work.

This is where you need to find out if a child has allergies, diet restrictions for health, religious, or taste preferences, etc. There are a lot of things that have to be considered when planning meals formally. We may offer up cereal to our own children for breakfast, but what do you do when little Johnny is allergic to wheat? Take a stroll through online forums or communities for some ideas!

Additionally, will you be using a nutritional program like those mentioned above? Will you charge extra and offer meals and snacks as an add-on to your rates? Make some decisions about this and then you will be able to answer questions and advertise accordingly.

9. ALLERGIES

I mentioned this in relation to the snacks and meals, but there are other things children are possibly allergic to. The obvious ones may come to mind: Bee stings, nuts, medicines. But did you know there are some other very serious allergies that are not as well-known? Make sure you educate yourself about the signs of a serious allergic reaction. Know the difference between a sensitivity and the onset of anaphylaxis. It's scary, but education can help.

Not only are many of them life-threatening, but sometimes the worst day ever can happen: A *new* allergy surfaces while the child is in your care. You can go to local health centers to ask about training on allergy awareness and how to recognize and handle an emergency. You may even be able to obtain and learn how to properly administer life-saving medications such as an *epi-pen* or other treatments. Parents of children with serious allergies put this absolutely first when choosing someone to care for their child.

Some allergies are less threatening but equally important to note. While you may not have to call an ambulance for hives, the last thing you want to do is return a child who is covered in them because you washed their hands with something they couldn't tolerate. Don't forget about Fido or the detergent for their naptime pillowcases!

10. PAPERWORK

Yes, there is a *lot* of it to consider. When I decided to write this book, I went to my mother, a long-time babysitter for her thoughts on what I absolutely must include. She always had several children in our home when I was growing up and they were my friends and felt like family. When I asked her about what she thought was important when starting a business as a babysitter, her *number one* piece of advice was, "Get it in writing." Get what in writing? *Everything*.

Not only do you want to establish a contract for your terms but you should make it fully legal. This can be done with a template or through some research and your own wording, but it is absolutely critical. When you accept a client, you want to assure yourself, and them at the same time, that this is a legal agreement. You will be available for them, and they will pay you *on time.*

You need to outline your policies about no-shows, sickness, terminating the contract, and more. Be very specific. When should they keep the child home? (Fever, etc.) When is it ok for *you* to call in sick? What if they are out for a few days, do they still have to pay you for that week? Leave no stone unturned. Read some stories online about unexpected or unusual situations other people have encountered and consider what bases you want to cover from the starting line, just in case.

You should assemble a standard packet that includes your contract as well as several other pieces of information and forms. You can set up your own custom form with several personalized questions such as: Do you wish for your child to be excluded from photographs during events or daily activities? Do I have permission to transport your child on outings or errands? Do you allow your child to play educational games online? Do you allow your child to watch television?

Really think about what activities you may consider doing through your day with these children and write them down. Don't worry yourself sick over it though, if you think of something later, you can just make a little permission slip per event or get verbal consent.

It's also worth mentioning your tactics for behavior correction. Is there something they do at home that's effective? A special phrase or process they follow that would be helpful (or that they request) for you to follow?

Don't forget the obvious standards like food/medical allergies, emergency contacts, permission to seek medical treatment in an emergency. A quick internet search will help you find a template if you are not sure you have all your bases covered.

These are very, very important. While we always hope for the best, you could one day end up in a courtroom for any number of reasons. Having these critical things in writing will help you and the parent keep the lines of communication clear and legal for everyone's sake. And most importantly, it will help keep the child safe and happy.

11. DISCOUNTS/OTHER FEES

There are multiple things to consider when it comes to discounts. You can reduce rates for those who stay with you long-term or if they have multiple children enrolled with you. On the other hand, you can also charge additional fees when you add services such as tutoring with homework, part-time rates for those who wish to remain on an as-needed basis, or if there is a lateness or no-show issue.

12. CHILDPROOFING YOUR HOME

In addition to the obvious plug covers and baby gates, you may want to think of some other things to prepare your home. If you don't have young children, you may want to purchase some essentials like a training seat for the toilet, diapers, pull-ups, little swimmers for summer, and wipes.

13. FIRST AID KIT

Bandages and antibacterial ointment are common but you should also build a kit that includes some other things. Health items like hand sanitizer (check with parents about this as it can be dangerous if ingested and some will not approve of its use), bug bite or sting sticks, and even calamine lotion for itching.

Remember to think about allergies when choosing cleaning supplies and sensitive skin soaps as well. You can start with sensitive formulas in the beginning or choose children's blends.

14. TOYS AND ACTIVITIES

There are wonderful lists online of suggested toys for various ages. You are going to want a small area set up for playing and that should include some items that will not only engage the children but also teach and be safe. Think about the ages you are planning to consider and build an area that is good for that range. Don't forget older children!

15. FOOD LABELING AND STORAGE

Snacks and meals are going to need storage. Part of safe feeding means knowing ingredients, dates, and keeping business food apart from personal food, so to speak. What you purchase for the children in your care (especially if you participate in a nutrition program), can be stored separately so that you have a quick view of what's available. You can also demonstrate this organization and storage safety to new parents and children on your tour!

16. TREAT AND REWARD SYSTEM

We think of how to curb negative behavior, but it's also important to think about rewards and treats for good behavior. Experts have demonstrated that using food as a reward system can lead to ill effects in the long run. With that in mind, it's a good idea to think up some ideas for reward systems that will encourage helpfulness and good behavior. From a sticker chart to a box of small toys, or activities that are special, having these treats available will be excellent positive reinforcement and motivation.

17. NAP AREAS AND SUPPLIES

Will the children you care for be taking naps? If they are at that age, you will want to have an area or system in place for this time of day. Structure is important and they will need it to settle down for a rest in the middle of the play day, even if they are tired. You will need to decide if you will ask the parents to bring bedding or if you will supply it. If so, you will want to make sure it is laundered frequently and stored in a secure way.

18. OVERNIGHTS?

Will you provide overnight care? If you do, you will want to make sure you have another set of guidelines in place for this special service. You will need to have a full understanding of what the child's usual bedtime routine consists of. Make sure parents bring all necessary supplies like pull-ups if needed, special sleeping items like teddy bears or blankets they are used to, and a change of clothes (just in case!)

19. LESSON PLANS

This is worth thinking about even if you're not formally educating. Your time with the children is not just about making sure they don't get injured. Remember that you are helping these parents raise their babies and that involves teaching. Think about age-appropriate life lessons and how to further what they are learning in school.

20. EXTRA CLOTHES

No matter what time of day you have the child, there can be a reason to change clothes. If you're dealing with a young child, you may have "accidents" to worry about. If the children are older, you could run into spills, messy crafts, or mud and rain. No matter what the age, there should be back up here!

21. DISCIPLINE

This is something you really need to dig into deeply. Not only do you need to be respectful of the child, but you need to consult with the parents about how they handle things at home. Children are creatures of habit and consistency is crucial. At the same time, there are certain lines you must never cross. You would think that it goes without saying but you must never lay a hand on a child for any reason, even if parents say it's OK. It is not.

It isn't about right and wrong alone, it's also about *the law*. Be smart and patient. And if you ever feel like you're losing your cool, *leave the room or call for backup*. Every parent would rather have a call that says "come and get your child, please," than to come home to a bruised child. Period.

22. GETTING PAID

There are some options here. There is always cash and even check or money order. But these days, everyone is accepting credit cards and there's no reason you can't do the same if you want to. There are many companies and apps that allow businesses and individuals to set up payments online. The client can go to your website if you have one and make a payment (your .web hosting company can offer this on some platforms).

Or you can set up an account through a company like Paypal and they can simply email you the payment! This can be as good as cash when you get a debit card from the company, which is offered to businesses. There are even little devices that plug into your phone so you can simply swipe onsite.

Whatever you decide, get this agreed upon with the parent before you begin caring for the child. Decide if they will pay you weekly (before or after the week), monthly or on some other schedule. There's no reason you can't tailor it to each client, but you can also set it so that your needs are the priority for dependability reasons. Some parents appreciate paying at payday twice a month or otherwise. Do what works for you.

23. BEHAVIOR MANAGEMENT - DISCIPLINE/REWARDS

It's inevitable, you're going to have children that misbehave. Even the most polite and sweet child will have moments or days when they're over tired, getting sick, or just down in the dumps. When the unavoidable happens, what will you do?

Talk to the parents about your ideas for these occasions. Make sure you are both on the same page and that you have several ideas in case one falls through. It's also wise to find out if there are magic words each child responds to, or if they are more likely to fall apart at certain times of day. This can help you keep things calm before they get out of hand in the first place.

Going back to the reward system, make sure your plans are balanced out to tell them they are on a roll of good behavior. Parents also appreciate little reports or certificates that show little Suzie had a super good day. And little Suzie will be very proud to show this to her parents, and feel encouraged in the future to earn more.

24. FIELD TRIPS

Will you take the children anywhere out of the home? If so, you must set up a permission slip just like in school. You should include your exact plans for the trip, a clear indication that you have permission to transport them, and collect any extra money needed if that applies.

You also need to make sure you have suitable transportation and supervision for an outing. If you are taking a few children to a crowded place, for example, you may want to consider asking another adult to join you. This could be one of the parents who might be available, or it could be a friend of yours. Regardless of who you choose, make sure all the other parents are aware this adult will come along and that they are OK with that.

25. OUTSIDE PLAYTIME

Nobody wants to be in the house *all* the time. But there are some things you will need to be prepared for outdoors. If it is cold, you want to make sure parents bring jackets, hats, gloves and extra shoes or boots if it's snowy.

On the other hand, if it's a hot day, you may want to apply sunscreen (make sure you have allergy information first!), provide extra drinks, and wear hats. If you have a pool, even a small one, you need to make sure children can swim and offer floatation devices to those who are insecure or still learning.

26. HOMEWORK

If you have after-school clients, you may need to get involved with homework. Make sure you ask each day and if you don't know the answers, look it up! Check with parents to see if this is what they want you to do, first. Some may appreciate it, some may not.

27. CAR SEATS AND TRANSPORTATION

Even if you don't plan an outing, you may find the need to take a trip. There could be an emergency or you may need to run out for something unpredicted. You just never know! This is why it's good to make sure you have both permission and equipment needed to do that if the need arises.

28. IF YOU HAVE PETS

Make sure to ask about allergies again here. And if the pet is large or the type of animal that could injure someone, have a place for it to be kept safely while your children are there. It's also worth asking the parents if their child has any pet fears that could come into play knowing the animal is in the house, even when it's out of sight.

29. MEET YOUR NEW FRIENDS

Invite prospective or newly contracted families to tour and visit your home. Not only will you give the parents peace of mind by showing them where their children will spend their time and how you store the snacks, but the kids will feel better for their first day. Having them visit during a regular day with other kids there will also offer a good chance to meet the new friends and have a plan for when they come back. They will get excited to return!

30. "I DON'T HAVE TO"

It's going to happen. One or all of the children will turn on you. Have the parents explain (possibly in front of you) that you are their new babysitter and you are in charge of them. This doesn't have to be in some authoritative way, but can be a quick sentence that you can refer to when the dreaded phrase comes out. "Remember what Mommy/Daddy said? I'm responsible for you so it's important that we work together!"

31. "I'M BORED"

This will also happen, for certain. And it probably won't be irregular. Kids get bored no matter how well you plan out the day. It's not just about having activities and a schedule but sometimes they just won't feel like doing your thing. When this happens, it's good to have little secret ideas to curb the boohoos. This could be a special movie or game, or even a secret healthy but delicious snack to change the mood.

32. LICE AND BEDBUGS

Yes, you can say it out loud. And you may have to because when you get into a social setting, one or both of these little uninvited guests can bring the family over, as well. Before you think about this one more second on your own, I urge you strongly to get your own information about the situation.

Lice and bedbugs are pests that can affect *anyone*. They are not an indicator of cleanliness but are almost always interpreted this way. Because of how they are viewed in society, they are extremely touchy subjects to confront. A very wise idea is to address it with parents from day one.

Provide them with information about the pests: How to recognize the signs, how to treat them, how they are spread. Make sure they understand that *you* understand this information and you are doing all you can to prevent the issues and stay aware of them.

You should also learn how to spot them and ask parents what their feelings are about doing regular checks of all the kids. Some people may be offended and you should have a back out sentence ready for that. "It's ok, not everyone is comfortable with that and I understand. I just offer this as a way to help make sure we catch them right away if someone were to spread it to your child at school or anywhere else "

Help them understand that no matter what, if a child has this going on, the family is simply a victim of a pest and you are there to help. What's most important is that *you* watch your own environment and get enough information under your belt to be able to say something to the parents if needed. If you know a child is dealing with this, you must be ready to ask the parents to keep them at home until it is resolved.

33. GROUP PROJECTS

Have some cool things going on that involve the group. The kids benefit from feeling like this is their home away from home and all the kids there are in the same boat together. Making art projects that you can use to decorate the environment can give them a sense of team building and group pride. This not only gives them comfort but reminds them to respect each other and be nice from day to day.

34. UPDATE LETTERS OR EMAILS

You may choose to take the time to inform parents about your day with their child(ren). This can come in the form of a daily or weekly update letter or email. You can also create a blog where parents can go to see posts about highlights of the week. This is an extra step but something that technology provides which wasn't available in past times.

If you're feeling really good about your uploading skills or tech abilities, a live nanny cam is a super idea. Just don't forget that due to privacy issues, this should be accessible only to parents and only if all parties are in agreement with their children being viewable. Get this in writing!

35. DAMAGE POLICIES

Sometimes kids break stuff. We all know this and it's a risk you take when you have children around. This is one reason to set up your space before you start your business. But sometimes it happens that an item will be damaged or broken.

It is wise to set up a policy in advance in case this happens but be prepared to address parents with unfortunate news just in case. Think about what's fair for them as well as for you. Is it the child's fault? Could it have been avoided in any way? Consider all of these things before asking for replacement costs.

36. PLAN FOR AN EMERGENCY

Sometimes you have a medical emergency and most people have at least a basic understanding of when to call for help or how to proceed otherwise. But there are other forms of emergency for which you should make a plan.

Weather emergencies are something we've all considered as a possibility, or even experienced. But have you been through this with a group of children in your care? Can you hold onto five toddlers in a tornado? You should know how to monitor the weather for potential severity and where to go in your house if there is a sudden turn of events.

There is also the terrifying idea of a social emergency. Many of us lived through the events of September 11th and we were almost all certainly caught off guard. It's not only a good idea to have a plan in place for your family anyway but you should also think about how the children you are caring for might have to fit into that plan.

37. DEMONSTRATE STRUCTURE

Having everything in place is amazing. But also pretty unrealistic as an expectation, especially for children. However, you should do your best to try for this every day. Make sure that you plan part of your day for after the children go home. Set aside an extra 10 or 15 minutes to clean up, get snacks ready for the next day, and generally reset the environment.

Children are known to thrive through structure and when they know they will walk straight to their red chair at the table for their snack when they arrive each day, they will be happy. If they walk in day after day wondering what will happen when they get there, the stage is set for insecurity and discord.

38. DECORATE YOUR SPACE

Take the time to set up the area for enrichment. Have lovely visual things present as well as classic ideas such as a famous print or inspiring quotes. This is also a great way to display art and projects from the group work mentioned above. Having your own art go up on the wall is very rewarding for a child!

39. KNOW WHEN TO CALL

Sometimes you need to call the child's parents. Don't be afraid to do so when necessary but don't be one of those people who calls for everything. This is a quick way to lose a client. People do not want to be disturbed at work but they also don't want to continually walk in to pick up their child who has been weeping continuously for an hour. If something is going on, it's better to just check in.

You may also find that some parents *want* regular calls. It's not the most common scenario but sometimes parents are uneasy about leaving little Johnny with a new person. Maybe this is their first babysitter, maybe they had a bad experience with someone else. No matter what the case, fall back to the respect the parents motto and make the call if that's what someone needs. It's not that big of a deal for you and it can make a world of difference for trust.

40. SCHEDULING DAYS OFF

Everybody gets to have days off, even the babysitter. However, you must remember that you are someone parents rely on so that they can go to work and do other important tasks. One idea is to make a monthly calendar for your clients. When you have an event planned ahead of time, do your best to give them plenty of notice (preferably a couple of weeks, minimum) so that they can make other arrangements. And always do your best to schedule your appointments and other errands on days and times when you are not supposed to be babysitting.

41. PROBLEM CHILDREN

No one wants to talk about it but sometimes a child may be consistently problematic. We can't always know what's at the root of it but there may come a time when you have a child who is simply too difficult to handle. The odds are the parents are going to be aware of this ahead of time but hope for the best. If this situation does occur, you will have to respectfully find a way to manage the situation.

The first thing to do is have a conversation with the parents. Explain that you have exhausted all of your ideas to control their little angel but are still having a very hard time keeping him safe and happy. Remember that if this is the case, they have probably heard this before and it may be upsetting or frustrating. Try to remain compassionate and see if you can arrive at a new plan of action.

If this does not do the trick or if you have a more serious situation such as an abusive child, it may be necessary to discharge the family from your care. This is not usually a comfortable situation for anyone involved and it is super critical the child does not come away feeling worse. Be sure to be polite and have this conversation in private, away from the child.

42. PROBLEM PARENTS

Sometimes the problem is not the child, but the parents. Maybe they are unwilling to work with you on payment schedules or bringing their child prepared for the day. Or they may be combative or accuse you of things as serious as abuse when there has been none. Obviously, if you see there is an issue that could escalate, or worse, already has, you will have to take action and discontinue the relationship. Always do your best to resolve the issue, but don't hesitate to protect yourself, especially legally, when necessary. This is not usual, but it's something to watch out for.

43. PACIFIERS AND BOTTLES

Know ahead of time what you are willing to manage when it comes to children who use bottles and pacifiers. Sometimes parents allow their children to use these past a time when you think it is appropriate but that is not your right to decide. However, it is your choice whether you are willing to take on the responsibility of keeping track of the pacifier, having backups, and making or cleaning the bottles. Special brushes and equipment are available to maintain proper sterilization of these items and you will need to make sure you can handle the tasks.

44. WHAT DO THEY WANT FROM YOU?

Know what the parents expect. Be sure that during your initial conversations and further agreements before you begin, that you know what the parents will want you to do. Go over everything we have discussed so far as well as new ideas you may have.

You don't need to worry about being overly careful as most parents will appreciate the thorough inquisition over someone who just nonchalantly accepts their child with no concern. It's as simple as "And what are you looking for from a babysitter at this time?"

45. ASK FOR REFERENCES

Hopefully, you will hear kind remarks and compliments from your families. When these days happen, take the opportunity to remind them that you would be very appreciative of a quick review or quote for your website or future clients. You could even offer a suggestion box or compliment box for them to anonymously submit to on the *outside* of your door so you can be aware of what you can do to improve, or where you are excelling.

46. HOME LIFE

You don't want to pry but it's OK to ask about a child's home life to a degree. If Sally's father has just left home due to a fresh divorce, she is going to need special attention and may be sensitive to talk about "what does your Daddy do for work?" at the group table. It's also important to know if they are dealing with any other difficulties such as the recent loss of a pet, struggles with leaving their last babysitter (what can you do to mimic something they enjoyed there?), or anything else the parents may wish to share with you. You are the professional here so just put the bug in their ear about it and see if they come up with anything.

47. PEOPLE WHO CANNOT PICK UP THE CHILD

While it may be another touchy subject, there could be people who are *never* permitted to pick up the child. You have the emergency contact list in your paperwork but is there anyone who may show up and should be sent away? If so, how serious is it? Make sure there is nothing fishy going on that you should be on the lookout for.

Sadly, this can sometimes be the case. If there is a true threat or concern and you decide you are willing to take this on, ask for a photo of the person in question so you can make sure you don't miss anything.

48. RENEWAL TIME

Yes, you have all your ducks in a row, but don't forget to renew! Make sure the parents are aware that you need to know about any changes in circumstance, such as address or work contacts. It's also important to just get fresh paperwork at the 6-month or year mark. Sometimes laws change or you may want to reset your fees for the upcoming contract period. You may have new allergies to add or different emergency contacts to use. Parents don't always think to remind the babysitter of little things that happen along the way so be proactive and give them the chance to just say, "oh, let's change this number."

49. DISCHARGING A CLIENT

One day or another the time will come to say goodbye to clients. It may be that you have decided to close up shop or it could be an issue that requires a discharge. It's important to outline this scenario in your initial contract with your families so everyone has a fair warning when a change is needed.

Children grow very bonded with their caregivers in most cases and it can be quite a serious transition for them to have things altered. When you have carefully considered all the avenues and have to end the agreement for any reason, make sure you have an exit plan in place for each of the possible scenarios.

50. DON'T FORGET TO BOND

It is last on the list, but absolutely number one. Make sure you bond with the child. Don't just take care of them, care *for* them. Remember they are having a great deal of contact with you and you have become a trusted adult in their life. You are teaching them, guiding them in so many areas of their life, and a new person they can count on. Make sure you live up to that not just in play, but for real. These are lives you are working with, not just a job. It can be whatever you make it, so make it a good time for all.

OTHER HELPFUL RESOURCES

Care.com - This is a wonderful website where you can list your services or seek out clients. The site offers background checks, profile options, and ways to communicate and even check out your clients before you have contact at all.

Pinterest.com - This is a site that is full of wonder. Do a search here for "babysitting" and you will be lost in amazement with charts, activities, first-aid, lists and anything else you didn't think of.

Daycare.com - This site is fantastic because not only does it offer licensing requirements by state, but it also provides a forum packed with information and chat. Go here to find out what you're dealing with before you even get started!

50 Things to Know

READ OTHER 50 THINGS TO KNOW BOOKS

50 Things to Know to Get Things Done Fast: Easy Tips for Success

50 Things to Know About Going Green: Simple Changes to Start Today

50 Things to Know to Live a Happy Life Series

50 Things to Know to Organize Your Life: A Quick Start Guide to Declutter, Organize, and Live Simply

50 Things to Know About Being a Minimalist: Downsize, Organize, and Live Your Life

50 Things to Know About Speed Cleaning: How to Tidy Your Home in Minutes

50 Things to Know About Choosing the Right Path in Life

50 Things to Know to Get Rid of Clutter in Your Life: Evaluate, Purge, and Enjoy Living

50 Things to Know About Journal Writing: Exploring Your Innermost Thoughts & Feelings

50 Things to Know

50 Things to Know

Website: 50thingstoknow.com

Facebook: facebook.com/50thingstoknow

Pinterest: pinterest.com/lbrennec

YouTube: youtube.com/user/50ThingsToKnow

Twitter: twitter.com/50ttk

Mailing List: Join the 50 Things to Know Mailing List to Learn About New Releases

50 Things to Know

50 Things to Know

Please leave your honest review of this book on Amazon and Goodreads. We appreciate your positive and constructive feedback. Thank you.

50 Things to Know

www.ingramcontent.com/pod-product-compliance
Lightning Source LLC
Chambersburg PA
CBHW030506220526
45464CB00006B/2676